Africa For Kids
People, Places and Cultures
Children Explore The World Books

SPEEDY
PUBLISHING

Speedy Publishing LLC
40 E. Main St. #1156
Newark, DE 19711
www.speedypublishing.com

FUN FACTS
about
AFRICA

The longest river in the world, the Nile (4,132 miles), is located in Africa.

Africa has the world's largest desert, the Sahara, which is almost the size of the United States.

Victoria Falls is the largest waterfall in Africa; it is 355 feet high and one mile wide.

Mount Kilimanjaro is the highest mountain on the continent.

Madagascar is the largest island in Africa and the fourth largest island in the world.

The worlds largest land animal is the African elephant.

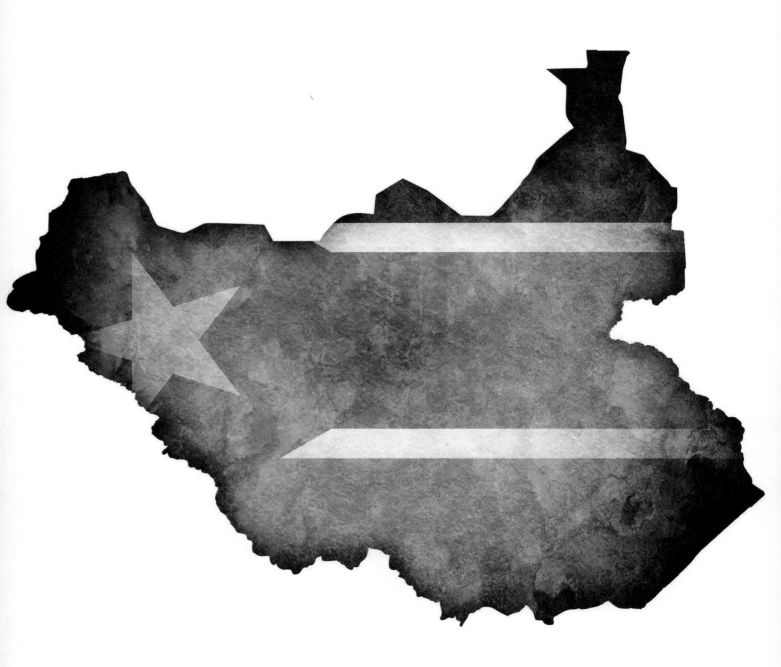

Sudan is Africa's largest country (968,000 square miles).

The African continent has the second largest population in the world, at about one billion people.

The largest religion in Africa is Islam, followed by Christianity.

Africa has the largest tropical area of any continent.

All of Africa was colonized by foreign powers during the "scramble for Africa", except Ethiopia and Liberia.

The Pharaonic civilization of ancient Egypt is one of the world's oldest and longest-lasting civilizations.

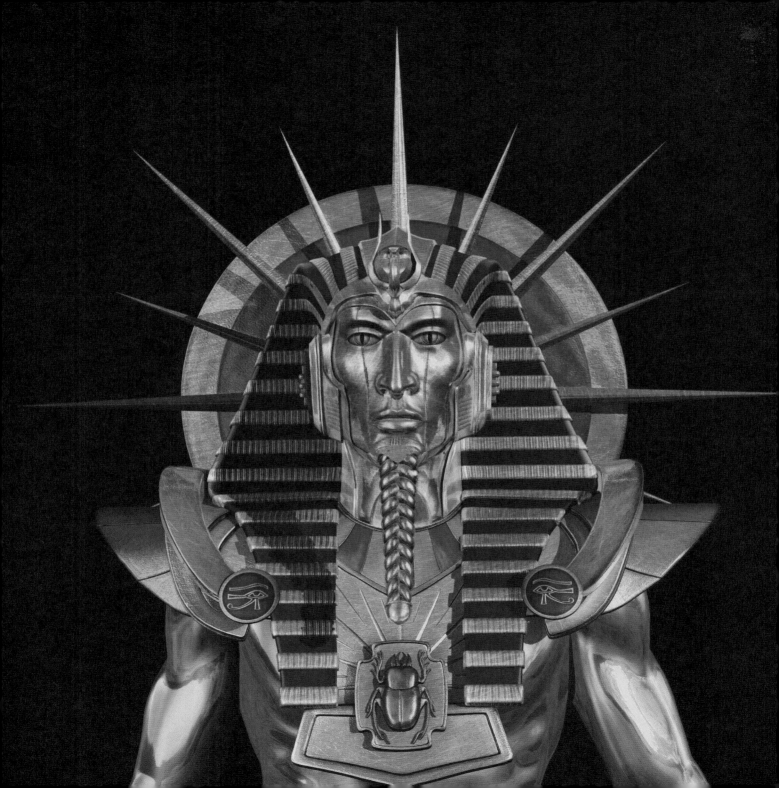

The Second Congo War claimed over 5.4 million lives and is the deadliest worldwide conflict since World War II.

China is Africa's top trade partner with Sino-African trade volumes now nearing $200 billion per year.

Over 240 million Africans suffer from chronic undernourishment

Lake Malawi has more fish species than any other freshwater system on earth.

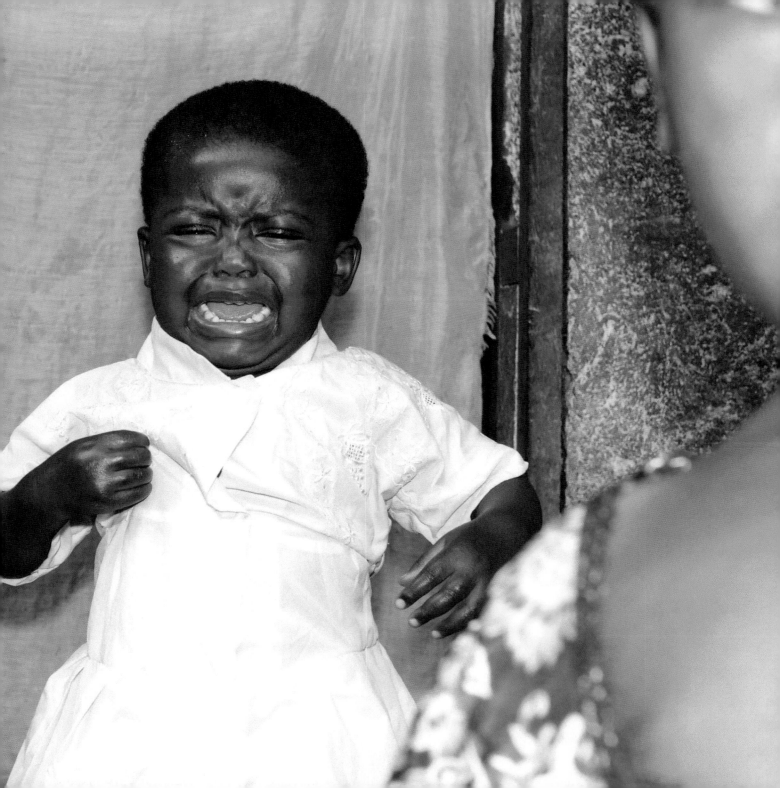

Africa is the world's poorest and most underdeveloped continent with a continental GDP that accounts for just 2.4% of global GDP.

Over 25% all languages are spoken only in Africa with over 2,000 recognised languages spoken on the continent.